Esther Becomes Queen

Storyline **Susan J. Davis**
Illustrations **Steven Butler**

Esther had lived with Cousin Mordecai since she was a child, but now she was leaving home.

The king had commanded that all the most beautiful maidens must come to the royal palace.

Esther's new life in the womens' quarters at the palace was very different from life at home.

Maidens arrived daily from all over the kingdom.
Each hoped to be chosen as queen.

Hagai was in charge of the maidens. Hagai liked Esther and gave her special treatment.

He gave Esther the best place in the women's quarters, special food to eat, and seven helpers.

All the maidens were given beauty treatments with special cleansing oils and perfumes.

After a year had gone by, the maidens were ready.
The king met one of them each day.

When Esther's turn came, the king liked Esther more than all the other maidens.

The king put a royal crown on Esther's head and made her the new queen.

The king declared a holiday. He held a banquet for Esther and gave out many gifts.

But Mordecai stayed in touch with Esther, and Esther continued to follow his advice.

Mordecai told Esther it would be safer if no one knew she was a Jew. Esther agreed.

One day, Mordecai overheard two guards talking. They were plotting to kill the king!

Mordecai told Esther, and Esther told the king.
Mordecai's quick action helped save the king.

Mordecai's good deed was written in the book of the king.
But time passed and people forgot.

Soon the king appointed a new prime minister, a court official named Haman.

Haman was a proud, evil man. Everyone was told to bow down as he passed.

But Mordecai would not bow down to evil Haman. This made Haman very angry.

Haman began plotting to kill Mordecai.
Soon he discovered that Mordecai was a Jew.

Haman decided he would not only kill Mordecai, but all of Mordecai's people, too!

But Haman didn't know Queen Esther was a Jew.
And he did not know she loved Mordecai.

Haman did not know that God was in control. God would use Esther to save her people.